Field Trips

At the Library

By Sophie Geister-Jones

level
2
little blue
readers

www.littlebluehousebooks.com

Little Blue House is distributed by North Star Editions:
sales@northstareditions.com | 888-417-0195

Produced for Little Blue House by Red Line Editorial.

Photographs ©: Wavebreakmedia/iStockphoto, cover, 15; Weedezign/iStockphoto, 4; FatCamera/iStockphoto, 7, 8–9; kali9/iStockphoto, 11 (top), 11 (bottom); skynesher/iStockphoto, 12; vgajic/iStockphoto, 16–17, 24 (bottom right); Stigur Már Karlsson/Heimsmyndir/iStockphoto, 19; Ridofranz/iStockphoto, 20; FatCamera/iStockphoto, 22–23, 24 (bottom left); EzumeImages/iStockphoto, 24 (top right); Rawpixel.com/Shutterstock Images, 24 (top left)

Library of Congress Control Number: 2019908616

ISBN
978-1-64619-030-0 (hardcover)
978-1-64619-069-0 (paperback)
978-1-64619-108-6 (ebook pdf)
978-1-64619-147-5 (hosted ebook)

Printed in the United States of America
Mankato, MN
012020

About the Author

Sophie Geister-Jones likes reading, spending time with her family, and eating cheese. She lives in Minnesota.

Table of Contents

At the Library

We go to the library.

We want to look at all

the books.

We find many different kinds of books.
We read the books with our friends.

We sit on the floor.

We listen to a story.

We laugh at the story.

The library has a dog.

We read stories to

the dog.

Library Fun

We make art at the library.

We use paint and brushes.

We draw lots of pictures.

We make crafts at the library. We use glitter glue. It is colorful.

glitter glue

We see a puppet show.

The puppets act out

a story.

We have fun watching

the show.

puppet

We play games at
the library.
We play mancala.
It is a board game.

mancala

Computers

We learn about computers.

We read books on

the computers.

We share our computers.

We wear headphones.

We listen to stories.

We have fun at the library.

headphones

Glossary

books

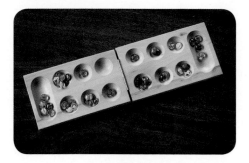

mancala

headphones

puppets

Index